ISBN: 9780997433647 (paperback)
ISBN: 9780997433654 (e-book)

Copyright © 2021 by Ormus Productions

Cover art by Kristin Farrell

Cover design by Eddie Vincent/ENC Graphic Services

All rights reserved. No part of this publication may be reproduced, distributed or transmitted in any form or by any means, including photocopying, recording or other electronic or mechanical methods, without prior written permission of the publisher, except in the case of brief quotations embodied in critical reviews and certain other noncommercial uses permitted by copyright law. For permission requests, contact the publisher.

Ormus Productions
East Taunton, MA
ormusproductions.com

Printed in the United State of America

First Edition

Publisher's Cataloging-In-Publication Data
(Prepared by The Donohue Group, Inc.)

Names: Burinskas, Michelle, author.
Title: Elysian fool / Michelle Burinskas.
Description: First edition. | East Taunton, MA : Ormus Productions, [2021] | Cover title.
Identifiers: ISBN 9780997433647 (paperback) | ISBN 9780997433654 (ebook)
Subjects: LCSH: Loss (Psychology)--Poetry. | Love--Poetry. | LCGFT: Poetry.
Classification: LCC PS3602.U752 E47 2021 (print) | LCC PS3602.U752 (ebook) | DDC 811/.6--dc23

10 9 8 7 6 5 4 3 2 1

Contents

Grains of Pearls	1
Jack Honey	3
Twilight and the Madman	5
Penguins Eat Mayonnaise	7
The Hummingbird	9
Fnu	11
The Toasted Owl	14
Clay Prisons	15
137 Lead Wings	17
Draw the Curtains	19
Summertime Masochists	22
#tremendous	23
She	24
A Sign of Life	27
Torn Shadows	28
Flush to Fold	31
Formica	33
Mock the Silence	35
The Woman Who Rakes the Beach	37
Prepositional Laments	40
Freeze Frame	42
The Eternal Equinox	44
Sparrow Hills	46
The House Always Wins	49
Maple Donut Night	52
A Turtle Crossing	54
The North Slope Oilman	56

Leaves Under the Hood	58
Elbow Room	60
Suddenly	62
Existence Petrified	65
Discount Carrion Petals	69
Toothpicks and Axles	71
Fragile Thunder	73
When Hemlocks Die	76
It Won't Leave	78
The Owl Theory	80
Sharpslot Road	83
The Spectrum Called	86
Never Enough	89
Mothers Without Children	93
McCarthy's Necklace	96
Break	97
Avenue F	99
The Shape of Waves	101
A Wrenching Cliché	104
The Lotus	106
Temporary Permanence	108
False Hope	109
A Final Inquiry	112
Weaving the Great Depression	114

Elysian Fool

For Doug & Cody

Grains of Pearls

She beckons the light on the darkest of nights,
then smothers the flame with a slice of her tongue,
leaving you stranded with nowhere to fall.
She'll laugh through her tears.
She's just a woman after all.

She'll bring you to life to pronounce you long dead,
then open her eyes while dreaming of your past,
rendering you weak as you're standing tall,
and blink through the nightmare
like the woman she is after all.

She sits in your shade so you might reach the sun,
then nurses the burns you were sure you'd avoid,
standing alone while watching you crawl,
and sighs through the sorrow
since she's just a woman after all.

She ardently lingers in a room without doors
for the astral return that may never transpire,
posing in shadows like a nude antique doll.
She'll trust through the lies.
She's merely a woman after all.

She fucks like an artist, and comes when she's called,
feigning the encore, she's vowed the long haul.
Her sharp screams are silent.
She's a good woman after all.

And when she is through,
she writes poetry for you,
whispering in her lilts and drawls.

Her love is eternal, her body ephemeral,
but you seek and find only what you can hold.
The blueprint is broken, obscene, and banal.
Still she carries your mistakes
as the idyllic woman and all.

She's like no one else, her road is her own.
Her ending draws near, and she'll set out alone.
Like light breezes turn squalls,
she's just a woman after all

And all that you'll see
is the memory of she
as she's before, after, and all.

Jack Honey

Even your body is just a place to stay.

And maybe you cry when you look at art,
while we bury our dead.
And a tear escapes the tissue
into a lap of guilt.
The shades of green are infinite,
reflected in the glass surfaces
as the black and white in prose
or the grays of poetry.
Another pour of whiskey
into a looking glass.

And maybe you cry when you drink,
while we gather in cemeteries.
And a sigh escapes your chest
into the empty room.
The shades of blue are endless,
consumed in audible aromas,
as the chords and notes of song
or drone of beetle's wings
that flicker as they sing
grave lyrics of the lost.

And maybe you cry when you read the news,
while we scatter the dead.
Their ashes swirl in gusts,
the wind escapes your grasp.
And the world slows.

The shades of clear are a chasm
of stories that ebb but never flow.
A tongue or pen on paper
writes the fractal screams
of American dreams
shattered on your park bench.

But you're a guest in every room you leave.

Twilight and the Madman

The sky threatens snow,
another bitter day
fallen into anonymity
as days tend to do.
A perpetual enigma
until night wraps its cape
around the moths.

Twilight's memento,
like laughter at a funeral,
echoes life's vanishing act
from the elusive white rooms
that keep our false secrets
nestled into the dust
all around us.

We lose the whole world
in less than an instant,
just as we receive news
we're all killing time
in a coliseum designed
by a madman who's tortured
by the ability to think.

He breathes in to exhale
while blood courses through
his crooked blue veins
chasing itself with a diligence
destitute of vision.

Soon the melee subsides
bringing his world into focus.

Let us not forget
to recall we're just mistakes.
Random medallions
sent to love one another,
shaping what we construct
for centuries on end
till our looming extinction.

But this opus is fraught
by grapples with death.
The elysian music
must eventually cease
before heaven's trap door
comes loose at its hinges
from those pushing and shoving
for their front row seats.

Penguins Eat Mayonnaise

Showing up uninvited at death's door
Time before the time after again
Picking the lock when it's open
The dependably aloof reminder
That nothing makes anything right

A closed garage and a silent exhaust
A bottle of pills and a liter of wine
A worn leather belt and a curtain rod
A silver blade and the will to let go
A loaded gun and no other way out

The familiar fumes displace the air
To the sounds of grinding machinery
Shrieking and catching until quiet
Save the guttural hum of the engine
Before it chokes in an ignition of life

The soothing rattle peppers the air
Drowns out the reticent noises
Pouring and draining each bottle
Consumed in emblems of the vacant
Before the purge stifles the binge

The white shower resembles a coffin
A cradle for suffering babes
Coercing and beckoning in waves
Of a curtain with the cinch of a belt
But the rod always snaps from the weight

The blood trickles diluting the sting
Coloring brightly the grays
Spreading and pooling outside the lines
Until it dries and then tightens
Before flaking off as life clutches itself

The magazine stoically waits
Holding tight its round of short answers
Proclaiming and framing simplicities
In its regrettable certainty
Yet the trigger won't be disturbed

All desperation and longing inspiring
These deliberate and feeble attempts
Prove what you've known all along
That despite a longing to succeed
You're perhaps only dying to fail

The Hummingbird

Flowers wide and sugar sweet,
she pauses for a drink.
In the flutter of a moment's space,
she'll waste no time to think.

A blood-red drop of Mother's ink,
she dips her beak into
droplet glories of dawn's stories
disguised as morning dew.

Her energy the speed of light
'neath the slowly fading stars,
casting trails through passing gales,
tracing every scar.

Her tint is not so brilliant as
her ever-absent mate,
but while he flits from bud to bud
she knows to sit and wait.

Her life's too short to waste a step,
on feet she cannot walk.
In blinks of eyes or sands of time,
the running of the clock.

This time's not meant for doing blind
whatever comes along,
for feeling contemplation's breath
suggests we could be wrong.

So move a million flits at once,
but never rush to do.
Learn from she and pause to be
since heartbeats are too few.

Fnu

Worrying her chain, she blankly stares
into the glare that's become her focal point.
A sun that once warmed now burned
an elongated journey. Inflated or reduced
to define the parameters of change.

The weeks of sickness bring comfort and fear.
Solid ground and home are distant memories.
Her stomach, a percolating center, rising as it falls
like their dinghy breaks the swells in defiance
of the approaching shoreline.

A passing cloud takes pity on her plight,
bending the sunbeams into submission,
so her vision might adjust to the dimming.
She finally sees what she's been gazing at.
A blinding vanity in the walls around the city.

Euphoria and melancholia conflict,
a war in her recurrent ruminations
as she struggles with elation and regret.
She escaped from her country on two feet
only to land broadside in a prison...for freedom?

Her voice that sang from her cell
through mundanity and conflict,
singing her children to sleep,
calling her men home from war,
will now be muted and shamed.

The irksome flare on the skyline returns.
She realizes it traces the horizon line,
awkwardly similar, yet completely different
than her old trees silhouetted the sky,
buildings and false institutions now in their place.

A hostile new home cultivates infirmity
and asking for help could perpetuate
her alien status. The breakers swell in reply.
Here, economics and politics trump humanity.
Under guise of asylum she'll become public charge.

Benefits dangle like rancid meat morsels,
poisoned apples that kill what they feed.
In seeking a refuge she's bound by deprivation.
She works, unwanted, in the bowels of plenty
while her temporary status hangs by a thread.

A man's hand finds her damp cheek
as she's knocked nimbly from stupor,

Get out.

And that rock of herself she once stood upon
in those moments eroded and, as she falls
in the wake of dismay, the dust washes out to sea.

Trembling, she stands in the swaying boat
willing her now-ancient knees not to buckle,
contemplating her point of no return.

Perilously, she dares a step forward not back.
The end of the beginning of the end.

She's handed a card limning liberty's spines
reducing her life to a tattered blue form.
Her vision blurs as three letters stare back.
Mocking her crossing they caustically read:
First name unknown.

The Toasted Owl

The leaves skat by
Unnoticed
The girl with the cup and no shoes
Beneath a lilac
Tinged sky
The fetid breeze their muse

From tap to tongue
It ran out
Upon his big head and small hands
Beneath an orange
Blue light
Flickering its harrowed demands

She stood in vain
A poor man
Wringing her woebegone thoughts
Beneath a heart
Blood white
Singing the troubles she wrought

Beneath a soul
Blistered
By pasts severed by what was not

Clay Prisons

Flicking off the things refined,
are revel heights in unclean minds,

septic thoughts in rooms aesthetic,
shrapnel from a fray synthetic.

Useless memories taint and turn,
and necessary stomachs churn.

Illusive rounds of bullets bring,
vague characters to which we cling.

Don't provoke the guns in public,
empty words we push to publish,

but our writing is a masochist.
Opinion's fact's blind activist.

The crooked saints are thick as thieves,
we feign our rights, roll up our sleeves,

cracking walls of frail clay prisons
that bear the weight of sins forgiven

until we reach a state of being,
a thin façade confined yet freeing.

When satisfaction's reached its brink
in bouncing heads condemned to think,

utopian lives, those fleeting figments,
stain our hearts with truth's sharp pigments.

We succumb to glasses overflowing
when they're empty without our knowing.

137 Lead Wings

Born on the water,
ensconced in the night,
she cried and then bled
upon love at first sight.
With the sound of your voice
rippling out in the air,
she'd bend and then break
to make sure you'd stay there.
Wrapped tight in a moment
that knows not to linger,
etching impressions while
fading out through your fingers.

And as her burning arms
long for empty's release,
she tries to escape
an ache that won't cease.
As men shift from boys
amidst shrapnel and chains,
the old missile silos
quietly collect rain.
Over years of remembering
what it takes to forget,
how it feels to hold you
without pleas or regrets,

she set out on the wind
who abetted her flight,
not from what you did wrong,

but all you do right.
Those that you touch
shortly bask in the glow
of an undying faith
in men that don't know
the meaning of love:
a bewildering maze
that she finds her way through
by your guiding gaze.

Her journey's one way,
a lone wolf unconcerned,
not fooling herself
over love unreturned.
But she'll lie in wait
for the rest of her life
to cry and then bleed
until you're by her side.
And if death finds her first
(it most certainly will),
she'll bend and she'll break
till her heart finally stills.

Draw the Curtains

There's an acrid old woman
who lives in a shoebox,
cries when she drinks
and drinks when she cries.

The guests will arrive soon.

Take down the torn pictures,
the bitter reminders
of what drew out the years,
the feigned truths we call lies.

She's preparing a sermon.

She strokes the black cat
who screams fickle demands.
"Companionship's cheap,"
cry his glimmering eyes.

Worthless mini croquettes.

Washing every clean dish,
she contemplates the flowers
she drowns just for fun,
her deft dismissal of time.

The old enemy lingers.

The phone's ring she ignores
knowing it always ends.
A cruel demonstration
of each connection that's died.

The mirror is cracked.

With each drag on the lead pipe
she dismantles a man
that she granted a glance
or dared beckon inside.

Coffee's at two, don't forget.

She revels in death's wake,
the only time that she smiles,
marveling at the knowledge
her time soon will be nigh.

Gone before their arrival.

She can't bear the clutter
in her head or this place,
so she shoves round the chairs,
a slow deliberate suicide.

The lost thunder consoles.

The world around her sleeps,
and she emerges to watch
the street lamps go dim.

She wakes at the falling of night.

Rains cleanse the empty room.

Her skin's lampshade thick.
Her will's wrought-iron thin.
She'll lock the door
and let no one else in.

Summertime Masochists

Lying next to the sun's counterpoint you feel a malaise.
Like a tick that crawls along your lower lid during sleep
making its eventual way through the duct,
only upon awakening to be discovered suckling
at the drowning soul's teat: the concentrically-pitted pupil
        peak.

Outside the switchblade grass ignites with fireflies.
The farmhouse windows cast vacant stares over the yard,
while street puddles sprinkled with stars ripple.
There are hands taking shelter from the dry darkness
begging their shallow waters to wash moonlight filth

from their cracks. The crimes of sun sleep flow forth,
impregnating stone walls that crumble with stop-gap
        redemption,
while you stand in your grave, above-ground, asking: Is it
a privilege to breathe atmospheres alive while the dusts
seek a death from shore through depths to distant shore?

#tremendous

This sound makes so much sense:
the strike of drum or horn
in downbeats of your heart
placing calls to newly born.

The sound affects the deaf
in sale of soul or pen,
a sharp resounding drone
infiltrating ears of men.

That sound in living color
erupts from pores to dirt,
while the self itself dissects
until even music hurts

as it builds chords into an opus,
brick by adept lazy brick,
till we're dancing between walls
forcing shapes where they don't fit.

Be still. Such chaos is the sound
in which silence must be found.

She

She walks the straight and narrow
biding her precious time,
but the line's a broken arrow.

The cat food and the coffee grounds
carpet her porcelain sink,
while loneliness confounds.

She paces slowly around the room
staring at the pictures
buried with her in the tomb.

She tries to see the faces
inside the wooden frames,
drawing in what time erases

from the cobwebs in her mind,
spun to hide the traces
of memories she can't find.

Sometimes through the sinewed folds
an image rips the fabric wall
to sculpt a false but perfect mold

that contorts the shape of things,
which persecute her dreams,
filling in what memories bring.

In bees that slowly slaughtered

a chicken bound to life
with little food or water.

They stung her legs and eyes
in afternoon's long hours
then methodically died.

She cannot bear to see,
yet cannot look away
from life's tenuous debris.

She wanders up and down the halls
searching for some relief
from the encroaching walls,

but as insult always finds
the site of injury,
a song cast her way unwinds

the pain its notes inflict,
leaving her to weep,
comforting as it constricts.

She pities her lot alone,
but through her sullen house
was the never-ending drone

of language plain as day,
scripting her heart's laments
in the most beautiful way.

A cold prison turns her home,
wrenching back the door
since these sorrows aren't her own—

her breath inside her caught
by this revelation
held hostage by her thoughts.

A Sign of Life

Your tears are not signs of weakness
They're signs you can handle your strength
Each day is a struggle
And life's awash in suffering

Your laughter is not a sign of happiness
It's a sign you're striking a balance
Life isn't a state of joy
It's a challenge of uneven weights

Your anger is not a sign of depression
It's a sign that you can love
Each day is frightening
And compassion's all we've got

Your fears are not signs of judgment
They're signs you can survive
Nature's ever violent
We must seek quiet from within

Your love is not a sign of acceptance
It's a sign of vulnerability
Life is fit with barriers
And the worthy break them down

Your sighs are not signs of resignation
They're signs of sleep starvation
Listen to your body
Each day is longer than the last

Torn Shadows

He holds onto a grudge until his knuckles are white—
Sees everything in destitute madness
when staring out into nothing.

He's a business man.
He's a scientist.
He's a politician.
He's a crook

whose cocktails are geared
toward humans.

Body and mind methodically atrophy,
and the apothecary tweaks his potion again
until he's reached torpidity.
The screams infiltrate the sounds
of life when he's alone. So what?

He screams at the devil.
He screams at the pills.
He screams at the walls.
He screams at the sounds.
He screams at the men.

Alone with the voices
on top of the mountain
at the very sharp edge of a cliff,
he tears off his shirt, ready to jump.

He swears he's fine
as he ashes into his coffee
prattling on about humanizing the masses
since 1972. But there isn't enough booze
to quiet the voices,
so he orders another round,
rocks in the corner, quotes the New Testament
accurately slurring
the words of his savior
for hours on end,
then paints nature scenes
on his eyelids
until he can open them again.

His eyes flash like knives
and his smile runs parallel
to a loaded gun.

He punches the window.
He throttles the can.
He kicks down a headstone.
He's barely a man.

The pills scattered, gravel
along the aisle he walks.
And the windows, dark and shuttered,
the light from the sun
a stranger
to a schizophrenic sky whose air shudders.
He believes it is infinite.
"So am I."

For all the gods' sakes.

The trails wind and pass,
leading up to a sun
he'll bathe in amidst the flames.

He's a parachute.
He's a wooden frame.
He's a cardboard box.
He's a paper plane.

A masquerading Icarus,
What does it mean?
He understands something,
yet in most disagreements
there is no quick answer,
as a door when it's open
presents every prospect
until it closes again
to become just a wall.

Still, to know is to opine.
In his psyche
nothing is free,
nothing is lucid,
nothing is pure,
nothing is fluid.
Even a thought
seeks independence from itself.
It's been mixed with something else
when his head comes unglued.

Flush to Fold

You're dealt the two and seven off suit.
The table begs a knock or shoot.
Heckling, the deck just laughs,
hiding its immortal staff.

You get one for free this time around
as you see the flop go down.
You stare at all the faces blank.
Your heart and club begin to rank.

Let's jack the ace beside the queen,
hearts on fire just like a dream.
You ante up for drunken rats,
wait for the turn to drop his hat.

The diamond king flips up and blinks
while the ace of spades just sits and thinks.
The ten must lurk among our midst
while you cling to hearts with dampened fist.

You call the raise for juveniles
while all eight eyes stare at the pile,
waiting for the rivers run,
knowing it's a mere warm gun

that all who play will wait to draw,
daring themselves to break the law.
A prison cell or groomed backyard?
Determined by that final card.

No longer pensive, he steals the act.
The black trump ace now settles back,
wielding his spade and taking lives
and breaking hearts before your eyes.

You cash in your chips, now left for broke,
admitting what the cards just spoke,
push back the doors of the saloon,
all your mistakes before you strewn.

Formica

I'm using a wine glass from my mother's china as an ashtray.
It may be a sign of the end of times.
Dogs in sweaters?
Tours of Chernobyl?
Self-driving cars?
Fuck.
The most versatile word in the English language,
can mean absolutely anything,
and it usually does.
Imagine
no longer feeling your extremities,
beside this rose-tinted, slightly-stemmed ashtray.
The warm throb of an animate rock.
A heart could suffice.

Drops of spit and merlot
against the breastbone of someone else's piggybank
stain a foreground of water.
A sign.
A symbol.
They're both typically ignored or mistaken
At the mercy of mankind.
My stain is permanent
and chemically pure.
A badge of honor
stitched on the back porch built by disposable trees
whose leaves bounce like blank rubber souls on ice.
The melt looks like tears.

I want to lift this ash glass or wine tray or window into
    another dimension
and smash it against the wall, the closed door, the terminate
    ceiling.
But I won't.
It's my parents' house.

Mock the Silence

The crippling self-loathing is more than you can bear,
and failure's victory dance is circling in the air.

The people blankly stare, deal shots in the arm for free,
offering empty smiles, feigning sympathy.

The colorful surroundings turn gray and overcast.
Dyes run in dried beds your tears had carved to pass.

The electric lights mock silence in that darkened place,
threatening the respite a wounded heart will chase.

The existence is defined as a long violent struggle,
an enigmatic test to see how much you can juggle.

The absentminded lemmings staunchly march ahead,
pausing momentarily to gaze through pools of lead.

The chambers in your heart and mind release the poison;
lava down a mountainside burning cheeks that quickly
       moisten.

The hordes go on without you as your molten rock feet dry,
and loneliness descends screaming, *following's a lie.*

The lone wolf is all we'll ever be in spring until the winter,
desperate, collecting moments in this vessel they will inter.

The single solace is the black cat who crossed your broken

>   path,
his message only that, *with time this too shall pass.*

The hopefulness is fleeting in his methodical long gait,
and time is the only healer, so all you can do is wait.

The earnesty in each paw's step gathers strength,
Hinting happiness' height makes up for what it lacks in length.

The Woman Who Rakes the Beach

Her cave is falsely lit,
in a world she does not fit.
With fluorescent glow
and prescription blow
she disguises her descent.

She pulls the handle back
mirroring all she lacks,
sees smiles shiver,
while his belly quivers
as she glances at the pack

of men who creep along
the line of sand and stone.
She swallows dissent
of their vile intents
and resumes her work alone.

She pulls the tool across
her body, full of loss.
Closes tight her eyes
drowning out the cries
from her haunting albatross.

She heads back to her lair,
finds powder sitting there.
With memory charred
she sniffs every shard
and collapses in a chair.

Fair trade blood diamonds?
What do I remember?
The dogs.
Man's strongest anchor to earth.
The most poignant?
Their wounds.
They never completely dried.
The feeling?
My heart.
Big heads held in such little hands.
Even my dogs were not my dogs.
At least not before they were Africa's.

Like a lion she wakes
and slows down for the sake
of adjusting her eyes
when she'll realize
even the camera's fake.

The rake lies like a corpse
discarded on a course
of hard work to save
her son's early days
riddled with remorse.

To him she would say
we miss things every day.
But we know everything
to which we desperately cling
becomes worlds in which we play.

Until they meet again
she will remember when
they would sleep starving,
mother and darling,
when he could on her depend.

Prepositional Laments

Writing poetry by candlelight over rye,
I hover under the spell that I'm under.
Where am I?

The bell jar looms over the bar where I sit
pressed up against the wood panels,
poor conductors of invisible channels
of ceilings below, floors down above,
and stifling walls all around.

I belong in the trees, beside sand dunes and seas
or flat out in the cacti, in canyons and stalactites.

But this room is where my whole life unfolds
inside this torturous house.
Through the cubes of ice I stare,
past the legs and the fumes in the air.
Why am I not missed?

A bleeding-heart liberal
and a cold-hearted conservative,
I'm stuck in the middle
Between, beside, and beneath,
but the tears down a cheek
always leak out the same.

Beyond that steel doorframe there lies
skyscrapers of hope and critical eyes.
Soon the curtain of platitudes will rise

revealing our sole spirit that lurks
from whence we came to when we die.

Freeze Frame

You lured me away from home
with smog and loose change in your pocket.
Now it's getting harder to breathe.
You draw me in like Harold the moon
with the stub of his violet crayon,
on an eternal search for your window.
I embark,
running, chain-smoking
until my lungs bear the brunt of my heart.
With the burn of each breath I admit
modern guilt,
built from the valley of the lonesome.

So let me down like you do,
sudden and easy
and I'll recede to the periphery,
and build an altar to the sun
complete with a winding stairwell
that leads straight up to hell.

Then, with lightning will and latent shame,
I'll run until my chest catches fire
or my body becomes an anchor of bones
inside you, where all is still.
I can barely breathe now.

I can hear the high and lonely sounds
in your voice—
the star a sky astounds,

the shoe a road confounds.

Remember
the spilt milk in rivers on the counter,
the towels set like stepping stones across the carpet.
But I'm not quite who I used to be.
You're exactly who you used to be.

One more rush of cold air affects a final collapse,
while I murmur cries that next time, *perhaps*.

The Eternal Equinox

The scent of dried leaves
rising from the dead
when the wind tears them up
from the ground

is enough to dispel
the dolor and doubt
off life's unprincipled
unbalance.

The sound of lost birds
suddenly found
when the stars settle in
to the dark

gather strength from somewhere—
an empty shell
that poses as boundaries
infinite.

The taste of raw meat
festering slowly
when the loneliness mocks
your farewells.

The tearing and gnawing
nudging us lightly.
Life clings to itself
regardless.

The sight of bare twigs
randomly scattered
when life can't hold on
any longer.

The feel of cold airways
conceding askew
when the seasons resemble
our sadness

could be the pathways
we choose not to take
for comfortable ease—
that old farce.

The rush of burnt air
rising to the surface
when you catch your breath
from within.

Take another step.
Endure the next moment.
All that's required
waits right here.

Sparrow Hills

A fight for peace unites us
in a front that makes no sense,
as two sinking ships set sail
at all passengers' expense.

The water starts to speckle
and drizzle turns to rain
and all our expectations
crash into glass panes.

The shag bark changes color
from white to gray and brown
as young men lose the war
and their bodies bloat and drown.

Patriotism hangs cloaked
in love and fear and blood.
It's marauding as a rat
escaping from the flood.

A mind's as double-ended
as a stick or coin or tale
of people blindly marching
till they lose or they prevail.

Dostoyevsky only wrote
because he couldn't speak
the stories of his brothers
in arms from cheek to cheek.

While a mother crouches over
her infant army son
to pick and rub and dress the wounds
from threats and ice-cold guns.

The weapons simmer softly,
emit a bright blue heat,
turning atmospheres above
our heads to empty streets.

From dead drops to the soldier
to children born into
a sandbox full of nightmares
their parents make come true.

Decades pass in empty threats
our rivals warn against,
and the cans of soup expire
while we mount our defense.

Our young will learn soon enough
To fight, hide, or run away
but never learn the value
of what happens when you stay.

While vodka runs in rivers,
banked by sledge and sickle,
down the hatch into their blood
in an enigmatic trickle,

the playing field starts blurring.
What are we fighting for?
The east and west bleed out
writhing divided on the floor.

Still our leaders execute
their desperate guessing games
without stopping to think
what we want might be the same.

In figurative air strikes
they scream, crumple, and lash,
blotting both our skies out
with black rain, fallout, ash.

This dust may never settle,
and we might not see the sun.
Blame human minds dead set against
admitting what they've done.

The leaves are weighing heavy now
with casts from stippled seas.
The drops that once held promise
now lithely spread disease.

The ocean's turned to puddles,
so peak into the chrome
at the anguished face inside it
pleading to go home.

The House Always Wins

His subtle eyes drench,
but before a teardrop falls
his system shuts down,

stoic and silent,
at the edge of a cliff side.
Creation's stuck here

without choice to be,
born to harmony's discord,
terrified to die.

Inanimate parts
of jagged jigsaw backdrops
play admonitions,

suspended gallows
with wings hung in the balance
on this empty stage.

There isn't a show.
The lead's gone before curtain.
Tragic comedy.

The shock's wearing off—
that affable drug placates
continuity,

now coming to grips,

dissecting, dismantling
the concept of "gone."

Each room he enters
becomes a mausoleum
of life turned to dreams,

of pacing the streets
collecting condolences
as time saunters past.

Moments take lifetimes,
a world that sets clocks by feel
while grief suffocates.

The hand he'd been dealt
seemed a gambler's good fortune,
but Luck feigns her clout.

Though up for a while,
dissolution reminds him
the house always wins.

Still, an existence
doesn't endure lengths and heights
in oppressive vain,

since the light that shone
through a curtain of darkness
won't be extinguished.

When loneliness creeps
into this heart turning stone,
memories ensure that he'll
never walk alone.

Maple Donut Night

He's running in circles
to make decisions in squares:
plaintive boxes
with aluminum sides
and ceilings of tempered glass,

the surface of which
reflects the burn of mediocrity,
attracts the adrenaline
arrests breath in its longing
since you were three feet tall.

She's running in stitches
making decisions in fabrics:
grievous tapestries serve
as carpet for walls
and paper for floors of unbound

fibers comprised
of sutures blending, dispersing
shifting shades in lines
and curves of complacent acuity
since you were two feet long.

Whether the mind
is arranged in cartons or cloth,
the shelter or shawl
keeps out suffering rains
defined by life's perpetuity.

And she'll color the world
in hues of pastel and gray,
synchronizing the hearts
of those who love absolutely
until we are all six feet under.

A Turtle Crossing

There are too many people here.
Taking.
Giving nothing but complaints.
Moving in, our belongings metastasizing,
until nothing's left.

The mayfly brings life
and then takes its leave.
But we're too quick to judge, discover, create, decide.
Ruin.
The final act in our uncharted symphony.

All the while, she slows down,
carefully judging, discovering, creating, deciding
before leaving no trace
on the tapestry dyed painstakingly,
gently stitched in violent weaves.
It lives.
Dies.
A harmony exquisite.

Don't touch.
Don't take.
Learn from the mistakes we've made,
as creation abides,
ebbs and flows
without claiming stake.

Her time-consuming swim to death,

to everything and nothing,
an undifferentiated wisp in the sea of nihility.

Leave it alone.

The North Slope Oilman

Rain falls in curtains
over the frosted mountainside
and his wise, weary, and woeful
ponderous yellow eyes.

He kicks the gravel at his feet
in absentminded rage,
cracking his back, emitting sighs
for the façade he's meant to save

from Her mild and measured hand
that sculpts the stone for free
with an arsenal of elements,
deliberate strokes he'll never see.

His arrival marks the bitter end
of a beginning apocalypse,
a drill holstered at his failing hip,
Her final creation now eclipsed.

Drawing to destroy this sacred habitat
for milk as black as night
injected into engines, eye shadows,
and most everything else in sight.

Finger hovering over the trigger,
another point of no return,
he pauses for a fleeting glimpse
of a stream watering a fern.

Reflecting, introspecting
upon the scintillating light,
a reminder that life's shown him
far more wrong than it has right.

The glistening snow's a blanket
that hushes sleep while mocking
the silence he loves like music
composed for Her to drown the violence.

The vacant sound is promptly shattered
in melody's eternal repose
musing, *Don't bury me. Scatter me
among the neglected and the stoned.*

Mixed with something else entirely,
stolen from the hands of Africa,
smuggled over oceans
to die in the oiled bowels
of the once untouched Alaska.

Leaves Under the Hood

He was old before his time,
a soul tinted sage
and a heart stained in grays.
No stranger to the torture
of the destitute days
strung together like beads
on a necklace of leaves.

And though anyone can play
a lone melody,
the challenge is harmony
to make deep the shallow.

From a woman who plucked
his sister and brother
from his side while he slept,
leaving him stranded
with the impossible task
of learning to forget.

But a memory's permanence
is a log in the mire
of cascading waters
every time his mind clears.

To a woman who sank
her claws into something
that wasn't hers to take,
tearing up hallways

and scars upon scars
just to say that *it's ours*.

Undoing the footbridge
he'd toiled to build
replacing it with minefields
and setting stealth devices.

And he never remembers
to watch where he steps.

She was every and all
things he didn't know
he wanted or deserved,
and though many had looked,
the first woman to see him
showed up on his doorstep
with food for the dog
and a throat on which to hang
the necklace of days.

And despite the truth
that he throws in her face
because he's not used to having
an escape from this place
she won't leave his side.

Elbow Room

At this juncture
we've nothing else,

but if what we can carry
defines us as men,

it might describe a woman
bound by contradictions

of a cosmopolitan
diplomat who prospers

in a country we made
inside a broken head,

crawling with termites
that slowly destroy

each pillared value
at its very foundation.

We'll give our spare change
but not the time

of day that is priceless
as the canvas we set

for the heads of dead men
on labeled currency

or events we stockpile
to define a great nation.

Seething with greed
and false paper creeds.

And the weather says
climates are changing,

as the trees catch on fire
and oceans flood with plastic,

we pop another pill
and watch the homes perish

from diminishing morals
and media stories

that tell us we're always right
on time for the show

starring the captain
of this sinking ship

whose bowels are filling
and spilling everywhere.

The chaos infiltrates
until we change the channel.

Suddenly

Caught in your riptide,
I'm still swimming,
choking on the foam
and breathing fresh air
for the first time in my life.

A flower in the desert,
my muse among men;
I'm writing at stop lights,
laughing through tears
that leave stains on your shirt.

You turn night into day,
settle the currents.
The bedlam inside
comes off course when you speak
catching all gone astray.

Triggering release
as the engine ignites,
backfiring the words
that now give me strength
but once made me weak.

I'm drowning and floating,
flying and crashing
all at the same time.
A victory in defeat
set from silently hoping.

Left kicking and stroking
while waves break all around,
I'm losing the battle
(there was never a war)
with the pierce of each sound.

You came out of nowhere
to say what I know,
It's complicated.
Is it? Or are we built
to believe life isn't fair?

Fourth degree burns
scorch my skin in the night,
sear from your absence,
blithe indifference,
your complete lack of concern.

I've got all and nothing
and am holding on tight,
eating to live,
drinking till I drown
this habitual sting.

I hope she brings joy
to your lake made of glass
where you've set her to float.
An ambient piece
in your dangerous ploy.

But asphyxiation
might be all our fates,
and the very last time
that I see your face
escorts a sudden
mighty
final
destination.

Existence Petrified

She
may be violent and cruel,
merciful and kind,
painfully gentle,

but never
ever
tether her
tempt her
test her.

She gave you life,
holds it in weathered hands.
She can tighten and take
as sure as her squalls
render stone to sand.

She's a scientist.
She's a deft artist.
Meticulously free from regret.
Full of purpose.

Precious lichens and crusts
grace her knuckles as proof:
in her devoted grasp they trust
as all have done before but us.

We approach on knees.
Reverently.

Respectfully.
To rest on solid earth:
her gorgeous marred and tattered skin
from which all begins.

The thought the rock could safely lead
is that of her greatest fool.
Her canyon mouths are yawning wide
the lips of which are labyrinths
swallowing both wolf and weed.

A single arch in red sandstone
poses as a landmark
as the North Star aligns a cinder sky
so mountains might call, breathe, reply.

Listening is an attenuated skill
that all her creation has mastered
save man,
whose arrival strains their survival.
And so few lives are left.

The music comes before it goes.
A floating ripple rings her call.
Dissipates.
The first step to being found
is knowing you are lost on hallowed ground.

Each step across her breast
transforms.
A lizard makes his way home

as a stone face painted mercury
becomes a river chrome.

Patiently productive,
she waits,
works away the ages.
Is it atonement or affirmation sought
when we snare her artwork into cages?

Juniper berries sway in schools
sprayed like stars,
her bitter jewels.
The coiled bark twists in climbs,
skeletons of pinyon pine
or cottonwood.

Blood-red, sky-blue,
agate transforms wood petrified,
perfectly preserved.

Disparate rice grass, fireweed, sagebrush
cosmically aligned in wait
for an unexpected
indeterminable
uncontrollable
Fate.

Quicksand floors,
her hidden trap doors
force desert rhythms to bend and cede.
Copper washes wind and stretch in mazes infinite

sprinkled with her turquoise seed.

Take care.
Take heed.
Footprints are never found in air.

The desert birds fly across the moonrise,
reminders that the sun's not gone but hides.
And we're left here to survive the night
to the wind's benevolent whistles and sighs
until her unfathomable wisdom decides.

Discount Carrion Petals

My little sister's smile is fatal.
It wasn't kind enough to rape her body,
but annihilated her insides instead,
slower than a snail squirms through mud,
leaving a diplomatic tumor in its wake.
Lungs corrupt the liver
in a strobe-lit system breakdown,
commencing a subtle invasion.
The cells' growth celebration
sound like slop buckets clinking in song.
Conditions and capsules fight
on her road kill-plastered streets,
while seconds elapse
over the yellowing fields.
The smoking-gun victim of
his consumers; sex sells
uncontrolled,
metastasizing,
morphing distorted drugs along
a pretty round face
through corporate whore glasses
for $7.89 plus tax.
The late stage paints the end,
drawing her near the edge.
Her flesh rots like sand angels
in dead winter breezes.
Gray eyeballs peak through
paper-dry lids
at a family extinct,

a system that failed.
Her pale cheeks collapse.

Toothpicks and Axles

They came disguised as a curse
in the yellow dead of night,
and when the moon handed you
off to the sun in routine,
a brief balance was struck.

Warm, wet, lost, and lonesome
they battled death's eternal grip,
clung to life's tenuous threads,
lost before they were known.
But the Darwinian escaped.

You were there to catch the souls
that cheated the weaker ones' fates,
to have and hold tight the fittest,
found and no longer alone,
to raise beneath a transient roof.

And as the reaper's contumacy
draws breath through its talons,
you stayed through the nightmares
staving off the anguish of solitude.
So they lived to see another day.

And for those that survived
there was joy, light, and love,
so when they left your side
they had the strength to suffer
all starvation or slaughter.

Know that given one chance
to escape their pallid fates,
running bush paths akimbo,
they'd cross a thousand villages
just to see you again.

Fragile Thunder

Some days
I miss you
So much it hurts
It's later on in those days
When suns kiss horizons
I remember the worst

One day
You taught me
To open darkness or beer
With fingers positioned
Just below the neck
When no one else was here

Some nights
When I drink
You come visit in dreams
Needing what you can't have
But I always give
Until I burst at the seams

These nights
I call upon
Our castle in mid-air
At the seeming same time
For when the heavens aligned
This immortal pair

Our souls

Intertwined
Knew what it meant
We could not be together
But would not march alone
Where our lives were spent

Your eyes
Ignite, overflow
And the streams that course
Across your soft cheeks
Stop me in my tracks
Each time I go forth

My heart
It succumbs
To a lyrical whim
Beating to the sound
Of your words breaking shells
To find their way in

You ought
To stop this
Dream of invented bliss
I saw you there in the water
Treading to nowhere
In a yawning abyss

Will you sink like a stone
Or swim through the air?
I'm no stranger to patience
In this blithe love affair

And there's nothing there
Save this magic carpet

In which each thread's a spell
That weaves among stars
To sounds of fragile thunder
Clapping bodies of arms

There lies a distant faint hint
Our heaven's in the air

When Hemlocks Die

I used to give medicine to trees.
They were dying.
Ever green they grew,
the first to stand on their feet.
They took notice
without complaint
of everything around.
Evolution runs her course,
and they watch,
sages among men.
Their needles give shade,
their branches a home
their roots till the soil.
Their souls proffer purpose
and air we could breathe.
But our presence triggered
a domino effect
mutating the earth,
we arose to infect.

Years of unparalleled art
stood as those peaceful warriors
that couldn't combat the siege,
so I set out to save them.
A delicate surgeon,
drawing up a sanguinary serum
with my humble syringe,
I'd drill through the bark,
split ages of rings,

that circular scrapbook
of every year's trappings.
Proof that there ever was.

In went the needle
through the ancient flesh
compressed.
Lethal fluids drained veins,
my last-ditch dose
to murder the pests
strangling the hemlocks,
the oldest provider
in the nature of things.

It Won't Leave

It can't go outside and will let no one else in.
It beckons a forged call that lingers within.

It leavens the terror from every warm body.
It mourns a past that glares vividly foggy.

It siphons veracity for a coarse distant lie.
It eats at her flesh and causes her soul to die.

It wipes, shines, and clears with a deafening purpose
until its face is reflected in every surface.

It wallows in a self-induced vacuum of air.
It drowns in the clutter the others put there.

It meticulously ignores the girls she inspired.
It deliberately tortures the man she's since fired.

It consumes her and frees her behind these four walls,
the only supports to prevent her fated fall.

It hasn't a name, a shape, or constitution.
It just fabricates problems all void of solution.

She has to leave, must pull it out at its roots.
It staunchly remains while her strength it dilutes.

She turns to the man whose stayed by her side,
begs his forgiveness for what she can't provide,

whose worn love breaks through a long acrimony
that waits deaf, drunk, and drained for her testimony.

It takes what it wants until there's nothing to give.
It severed all faith, hope, and will left to live.

Will it let her go on or consume her forever?
Or extend its firm grip round her throat, whispering,
"Never."

The Owl Theory

We sit at a crooked table
playing a game we cannot win,
fighting with the judge against
a false sense of innocence.

We're chained to fictive freedoms.
Birds bathe in a slanted pool.
A false sense of cleanliness
or scant attempt to stay cool.

Long wavelengths split, refract
upon a splintered sea of glass,
casting a false sense of brilliance
in fractured colors of the past.

The brittle fraying filaments
form the beings we possess,
a false sense of fulfillment
unravels until there's nothing left.

We're crossing the burning bridge
over roads heaving till they crack
with a false sense of security,
knowing we won't make it back.

Our clothes hang in mock defeat,
exposing our abilities—
flags of shattering divorce
or false sense of stability.

So we march deformed across
scratched court floor firmaments.
We reach the witness stand
with a false sense of entitlement.

We testify in perjuries
while we fatally bleed out,
but all our blood turns red
beyond a reasonable doubt.

Children move into their cages.
The unguilty pay a penance
as the system wields her staff
with a false sense of benevolence.

Our phones will hide the glare,
shield our eyes from shifty business
our smug leaders carry out
for a false sense of happiness.

We just stand there and complain
behind the walls we built around
a false sense of immortality,
then we watch them crumble down.

We test antiquated theories,
affecting tragic actions,
just to fall asleep at night
with a false sense of satisfaction.

Behind months of sober trials
the prosecution finally rests,
and a gavel meets the stand
in a false sense of justice.

It's ever harrowing to be
where ocean meets the land,
a false sense of gratitude
engulfs every girl and man.

Sharpslot Road

We could learn a lot from bees.
Each individual practices the art
of unimportance,
toiling for the sake of a greater good.
The death of one matters not.
A nomadic army swarms
to her civil symphony.
Their work is not prideful or lazy,
but hard and humble.
With each buzz or bumble,
they serve till their final breath.
As the synergy of flower and bee,
apple and man,
you and me,
it's our responsibility to practice striking
a balance.

We'll turn to dust soon
enough.
Every problem is a solution.
Every answer becomes a question.
The infinite insanity
still murmurs,
We're almost done here.
So stay awake.

Like a whale in open ocean,
happiness escapes us.
He'll swim without bounds,

as the moon draws her ellipse
alone.
Her two craters cast down
in sorrow,
while a third lays agape
at what the other two see.
Her skull, cleaved in agony,
is completely round despite the melee.
Her memory stretches far
because she feels every thing.

Age works like a sorcerer's case,
a futile chase
turning reality into dreams.
And blissful ignorance slips away
like sand through clutched fingers.
So stay away.

The manic leopard paces his lair,
moans from the outside in
until there is no sound.
The sighs and songs of the night,
just a moment here or nowhere,
sets a sky alight with lover's wind
leaking from the swollen clouds.
A mist or a flood confounds
his dying with each leap and bound.

Meanwhile, it is us who lay stake
to a ground we can't take
by kitschy anecdotes or American beauty,

looking down
from the top of the food chain.
We were all meant for this,
amidst nuzzle and fist.
Respect the rest,
lest they cease to exist.

The Spectrum Called

You greet the day like a guest
in a motel room,
a complementary mirror on the pillow.
But you're still short a buck
and your girlfriend's been late for days.
Ever a soldier, you armor up
in Beetlejuice's beauty
and Daisy Buchanan's brains.

The trees can't bear to share ground with you,
yellow with nausea
they begin dying their thousandth death,
flooding the air
with carbon dioxide
when you're near.

You've been drinking and shouting,
and the crowds all scattered
suffocated
from the reek on your breath.
Offensively ignorant,
conscientiously sincere,
indulging futility
Why are you here?

You cultivate insanity.
Your cause is deliberate
yet there's no rehabilitation for imprudence,
so we suffer and pour you another,

wiping up powder for hours
never daring to underestimate
the reach of your powers.

Your words slice like knives
in sheaths of misconception.
You're right twice a day
like a stopped clock,
considerate of nothing
guilty of everything,
and the prosecution is imminent
ominously waiting.

But the shed's full of weapons.
Obliviously you snatch
the shovels and blades,
slicing and dicing
the wood of dead trees
to build your labyrinthine ego
into a maze of closed doors,
until you've constructed a psyche
upon which no one can depend.

And we carry that weight.
You talk through the questions,
have all the answers
and could count on two fingers
the times that you listened.
You find quiet introspection
a fatal disease
and vaccinate daily

with all the insults you please.
Still, loneliness is the only reply.
How are you doing it?

What are we doing here?
Exchanging pleasantries and weather reports
until you become the assassin,
firing away until I spin away
from inside my head.
The smallest blow of your tongue
and I fall to the floor
bleeding out through my temples.
And I gave you the money for those bullets.
I cleaned the gun.

Before I go,
let's talk more about what we're not saying,
watch the rug bulge and split
from years of its swallowed lies
diluted with dirt
swept up in neat piles
shoved into their refuge
never to be seen the same again.
We'll confront some permutation of them
when we clean the house.

Never Enough

You walked on my fragile side.
Each day we heard the trains.
From between my legs,
you watched the world go by.

Listening to Knopfler tunes,
string after string of folk
walk to us in purgatory,
their heads deflated paper balloons.

We strode along the water line
on our way to that ocean grove,
in our sacred earthen home
two spinning worlds collide.

Sitting with you, pain disappears,
the world scintillates
in the smoke of a crumbling chimney
turning back the years.

I know you're not enough.
Would never be enough.
And though we lay across the tracks
blankly staring at the bluffs,

the air misted in silver shades
while we were on the railway
just waiting for the end
or beginning of the day,

this restless mind chants
droning satisfactions
lying just beyond my reach.
You broke the wicked trance

forced me to stand upright,
picked up the sharper pieces
recovering just enough
to make it through the night.

All the mornings I struggled,
the sun's invasion left me
paralyzed until you pulled me out
on solid ground before I buckled.

I crawled after you each time.
Your deft spirit made a home
for mine to recover from the road
where anger left me blind.

You taught without limits,
both flora and fauna,
spreading peace amidst mayhem
in the sad space space inhibits.

I wanted you for my own,
but you were the whole world's.
Your powers were boundless
evinced in branch and bone.

Other times you'd just sit back
and watch the world burn
because saving it was futile
with a rope that's nothing but slack.

I couldn't carry it all
and neither could you,
so your lids would grow heavy
and I'd rest as you'd fall

asleep to chance on the wind.
We dreamt of the days
that we'd grow older together,
but our time would grow thin.

And the curtain soon fell,
shielding a vigilant gaze
as you cast up to the sky
and my ground turned to hell.

The dirt and the tears
dried and caked red
where I shivered and broke
until the air around cleared.

As all things, you passed by.
Now I stare out into nothing,
left with this old guitar
and a dim rose-gold sky.

Your ash remains in a pile

scattered out in the yard.
I put a swing there to visit you
every once in a while.

When this world is too much,
and I'm sure I will perish,
I look to the place you changed,
feel your gentle touch,

and it seems to stave
the thickening burden,
while light beams hold on to
the life that you saved.

Mothers Without Children

We live like we have more time,
taking advantage for granted
until we're left sprawled
on a ground that disappeared
from underneath our feet,
while the sky concurrently caved
in on our fragile heads
drenched from the tears
that fell down in fathoms
with such ineffable force
that no sound could escape.

All we crave is escape,
a respite from the wrench
nestled between our breasts
slowly turning the organs
into disrepaired tissues.
Explosions inside,
the interrogation techniques
we carry out with insolence,
indulging hollow scrutiny
when the heart plays the part
of sadist and masochist,
cross-threading the screw that
held the whole world in place.

This place is an icebox,
the chill an oppressing, opaque,
constant old friend

infiltrating the scenes
projected in secret corners
of our rooms without walls.
The elusive doors to which
only we hold the key.
And as the frost slowly creeps
into these spaces, we recede
into meaningless phrases
since respect for our grief
is a torn paperback novel.

A novel anachronism
comes spryly undone
when the funeral is over
and not even crickets
can be heard over the drone
of the unbearable silence
blaring declarations.
We're stripped and alone,
not for the first or last time,
but the worst simply since
we have no choice but to figure
out how to go on without them.

Without the children.
We call ourselves mothers
having sat at their bedsides
as they absolved their short life
leaving us within barely
an inch of our own.
Their suffering ended

when ours really began
and since our time here is bleak
perhaps we'll try again.
Though each convalescence's the same
acclimation to loss,
a burlesque crude notion
emblazoned over and over
on the chests of the pitiful.
But what the hell?
We've nothing but time.

McCarthy's Necklace

Election time is infection time.
Humanity's too well hung.
Not strings of balls 'round human necks,
but shards of glass dangling featherlike,
tinkling softly beneath a nightmarish web.
Existence,
the native dance of bloodless love to a violent pulse,
and he's broken all of their legs
beginning with the snakes.

But man is always surfacing,
connected to her energy.
Oblivious,
until the glassware shatters
and he can stand on the rock of his lungs again
with rattling breath.
A race of men
can hope for nothing more than a slivered crescent moon
hanging on the darkness.
Still.
Her magnanimity confounds.

Break

The trees are creaking,
their leaves long dead
as branches brush the sky.

Still gnarled, reaching,
poking pinholes
across the blue of night.

You only see them
with sun's retreat
beneath the severed ground.

When worlds drip darkly
the light seeps through
those hollows nigh moon's frown.

Bright voids glisten,
we call them stars,
ignite this absent space.

Yet some consider
these rips and tears
deformities of grace.

Alone and crowded,
we swallow loss,
search for a path in vain.

That faint starlight glow

could be for some
enough to ease the pain.

Avenue F

Set adrift on a sea
of deceit and infidelity,
lost in cemeteries
filled with gilded memories
of you.

Shooting synthetic stars
teaching the unmastered art
of unfettered kindness
leaving those willing blindness
to drown in their tears.

Your lips twist, spin a cloak
of invisible smoke,
mirroring your septic heart,
black as white in the dark.
Leave me alone.

Doing anything but nothing
to drown out the something,
not to think about thinking
we were forever sinking
since you can't float.

That farce of permanence
stains a lovely instance
when forevers pervade.
Every little thing fades
so let go.

Still, a broken blueprint guides
us weary down tunnels lined
with lethal temptations
all converging at stations
that collapse.

Our last attempt on a clean slate
you shy from love, prefer hate,
until heartbreak or death confounds
and the body and mind compounds
in the grave.

The Shape of Waves

In fear it trembles,
from joy it shivers
in scintillating flecks of broken light.
It refracts in rainbows
from bent beams of days
with outreaching rays of hidden nights.

In substance it confirms
what life seeks to retract.

In science it's studied,
in artwork portrayed.
Poignancy forms redundancy,
abiding ebbs and flows.
Its frequent wide lengths
swell abundantly.

Ambling along,
whispering, swaying
through skies turbulent, composed,
until one fated day
into the formless
the form leaps deposed.

Waves meet the land
in prisms and sand
and it simply disappears.
Her deft sleight of hand
purges in an instant

all evidence it was here.

From out of nowhere
it crashes on the beach,
splintering droplets that vanish,
becoming just a memory
burned in the mind
the world seems to have banished.

Still, the water remains
streaming now without shape,
raising creation,
eluding destruction.
The spirit can't escape.

So when I lost you
I sat down by the shore,

called upon this image
through blue eyes sealed tight
letting peace infiltrate
the deafening discord.

I watched the shape of waves
crawl, crash, rescind
as they have done
infinite times before

until the tears ceased their torrent
and joined you at sea.
I let the winds dry my cheeks

and soothe every sore.

Wrapped in your presence
I came to terms with the fact
that I could no longer
hold you close anymore.

Yet, you're here all around
as you always have been
and always will be.

Nothing less.
Nothing more.

A Wrenching Cliché

It ended before it began.
Lost before it was mine to lose.
A summer deep in the woods.
I'll always remember us this way.

Your love was tenderly vapid
and the fall was steep.
There was nobody else
to cushion the fall.

You invited me from shadows
to this divine empty house,
but then you walked out
and I woke up alone.

You helped me build walls,
but I'm no architect,
so I try not to laugh
when they predictably crumble.

Folding laundry with wine,
lost in useless thoughts:
for you, I was disposable
as a junkie's bent needle.

I can't help that I miss you
or who I was beside you.
When you caught my spirit,
I never thought you'd let go.

Your gaze settled on me
and burned me alive.
I emerged from the flame,
better off—but still ashes.

I'm fractured, distracted
and your eyes fix to destroy
while mine flood with the loss
of what can't be replaced.

The sun stained the nightfall
so we could see for miles,
and though I saw the clouds forming,
graying a lavender sky,

I couldn't predict the rain
would come down so hard.
I thought we'd change the world,
but it changed us instead.

Forever's nowhere around
when the end rears its head.
You stole everything you could
when I had nothing to give.

My beauty's easy and thrilling.
Yours, progressively arduous.
So hand me that wrench.
I'll always remember us this way.

The Lotus

You're an idiot for losing her;
the most beautiful person
kneeling before you,
yet staring from above

with startling eyes,
windows to the prison
supremacists like you
have built around her.

Her curves form a cycle
of victorious defeat,
an ouroboros whose inside
was dyed every shade of blue.

Heard before your advent,
readied for the fall,
she opened old wounds
clutching needle and thread.

Circumspection constricts
movements and logic
as she plays the victim
in this obsolete church.

Misogyny flaunts
its pedigree of false light,
though she's found it quite painful
and has learned to close off.

It's celebrated in you
when censured in her,
whether malady or opinion
it's a counterfeit contrast.

But when she looks up
at you from the tower,
you shrink down confounded
by her steadfast acuity

to change your rigid mind,
post your overdue bail
from the lifelong deception
that she must be saved.

The rock that you stand on,
her uncivil disobedience
will render you whole
or bury you deep beneath it.

That's what she looks like,
in hopes the light remains dim
so no man will see outside
but instead what lies within.

Temporary Permanence

August fades to autumn.
Leaves shift from green to gold.
The assassin frost awakens,
a lesson in letting go.

Clouds bleed out in protest,
flanking lines in violet hues.
The sun stains an earthly ceiling
as she bids farewell her muse.

Black circles wreath his sad eyes,
and his corona stretches wide.
Moonbeams cling in desperation
to the elusive edge of night.

Pressure falls constricted,
nude airs swallow whole the mire
while paling mist in leaf and limb
seems to set the world on fire.

The city builds a tower
with desire and hollowed bricks,
and since our loneliness restricts
the time bomb patiently ticks,

and we're shattered when it falls,
though we know it was born deceased.
Falling air and sunset moons remind
pain subsides upon release.

False Hope

I thought you should know.
You did it again.
Broke it back open
after I'd spent a year
collecting reflections,
rotating the shards
until they slid back together,
so that I could maraud
as a whole wishing stone
strongest at its cracks.

I thought you should know
I don't travel light.
Moving with the world
balanced in my head,
the one that you cradled,
barring those dire days
you disappeared into silence
when I held it for you
safe from the fire
you'd set and watch burn.

I thought you should know
you are all I can see
at the bottom of a glass
or a mirror's rear view
or every desperate time
I will my eyes to close,
begging slumber take me

away from this place,
a long-shot fleeting break
from the picture you painted.

I thought you should know
the very last time
was the first time I saw you.
And I nearly collapsed complete.
We sat on the floor
surrounded by windows
through which stood a man
I had not met before.
Your words were my downfall
then, between and now.

I thought you should know
I had you pinned;
A lone star, wolf, and worker,
stoically listening
to loneliness cries
from our heckling minds.
Against better judgment
I plowed full-speed ahead,
blinded by the thought
of life without you in it.

I thought you should know
I can't take any more.
I'd find heaven for you,
lay it down at your feet
shorn of strings and stipulations

for your distant grace.
But I've reached the beginning
of what won't seem to end,
so this fractured heart
will spend seven lifetimes
letting you go again.

A Final Inquiry

It's thinking of twilight, the end of September.
I'm calling you now just to help you remember.
The sky's turned to gray but she likes what she's spinning,
a tale on a loom or lie piercing the evening.

I hear you breaking your self-induced limits far down the highway.
You're running from nothing now.
I hope you're building some sort of segue

since Syd sent for the broken and lost,
her mirrored self in their eyes
from all that you left or forgot.

The last time I heard you your voice sounded thinner.
I assume from the bodies you'd told not to linger.
She'd been to the pillbox to mark every day,
but awoke each hour to a thickening haze.

And you shattered that woman within an inch of her life.
And when the pieces came back, they were nothing but knives.

So, forgive me, but why did you waste so much breath
inhaling the wind from her sails
until they carpeted depths?

Now I close my eyes and you're there
ransacking freak shows and fairs,

while she'll scrutinize all that she tried
to see inside your bars from the outside.

And your arms were the house she'd been trying to build.
And it burned,
flashing silent farewells.

And the world around stilled.

I suppose, if you come around here
for Syd or for me,
I may return, but our dearest has gone to the seas.

She's become the broken and lost,
her mirrored self in their eyes.
But I'm certain you've left. Or forgot.

Leave a message.

Weaving the Great Depression

You drove me to that broken home
but weren't the one to pave the road
lined with mines and one mirage
(our broken, cut-up film's montage).
The potholes and the weathered pits,
scars of war's glamour and glitz,
a gimp's tactful stepping stones
led to a holy valley growing bones.

And we consummated ages
of reticent shifts and turning pages,
unspoken words the only sign
of what was yours but never mine.
My languid heart, a paper plane
and your brisk touch an open flame.
Sharp words twinkled, hung in spite
across chilling silences of night
where my eyes would bulge and creak
waiting for you to fall asleep
when I would dream of soon's before.

And your book pile by the door,
my companions when I woke
from nightmares where we'd not spoke.
This sharp quiet renders me deaf,
dreaming of leaving nothing left.

Deft knives that carve their tales alone,
the greatest story you'd ever known,

as agate infiltrates a wood
leaving it petrified for good.

After too much time, Mr. Jones,
for you I became a stone.

Acknowledgements

I'd like to take a moment to thank all those who made this book possible. From inspiration to input, the following individuals have my eternal gratitude. Bill, my partner in publishing and one of my dearest friends, is a true patron of the arts and the only person I know that makes six figures and lives paycheck to paycheck. Thank you for always believing in me and my writing when my beliefs faltered. David, another dear friend and fellow writer, your feedback throughout this whole process made this collection more powerful (and a whole lot shorter!). To my sisters, by blood and by choice, Christine and Kristin. Your true beauty and genuine goodness inspired so much of the love and hope that runs through these poems. I hope they serve to lift you up as your artwork has always done for me. Jimbo, my kindred spirit and close friend, thank you for coming back into my life in time to extend your wisdom and support to my writing. And finally, to my editor, Sarah. I feel as though your name should be beside mine on the front cover of *Elysian Fool* for all the work you did on this manuscript. Working with you has made me a better poet. From the bottom of my heart, my sincerest thank you and deepest love to you all. And also, thank you, Chris Raymond.

About the Author

Michelle is an ESL teacher, writer, and editor who has worked in the realms of poetry and prose for over twenty years. Her appreciation for art has been inspired and cultivated by music and writing, as well as her travels across Zambia, New Zealand, the Dominican Republic, the American Southwest, and her New England home. As she believes Mother Nature is our greatest teacher and the most brilliant artist of all, she spends most of her spare time outdoors and at the beck and call of animals.

www.ingramcontent.com/pod-product-compliance
Lightning Source LLC
Chambersburg PA
CBHW030449010526
44118CB00011B/859